Free Running

Contents

Written by Andrew Fusek Peters

Collins

Free running

Free running is a sport where people aim to move from one place to another with **obstacles** in between. It's like gymnastics, but practised outdoors, using buildings, roofs and rails. These **stunts** are both dangerous and impressive. Free running is not only a sport but is also used in films where such stunts are part of fast-paced chase scenes.

The challenge of free running is to perform the most difficult stunt while making it look easy and smooth.

a free runner leaping through a gap

3

David Belle

Free running began in France with a boy called David Belle. His father told him stories about his experience in the French war in Vietnam and how he kept fit by using a **military** obstacle course. His father had used the exercises he'd learnt from the obstacle course, such as leaping off high structures and **vaulting** horizontal poles, to hide from Vietnamese soldiers in the forest.

soldiers training on a military obstacle course

4

As a teenager, David wanted to see for himself if he could fly from branch to branch in a forest or leap from buildings and land on the ground with a forward roll. He then changed the military exercises to make them work in the city. Instead of jumping and leaping around an obstacle course, he wanted to develop new moves that would work in the streets and buildings of the suburbs of Paris. He began to train with friends.

But free runners can't just start by trying moves out in the streets. It's important that they practise and develop their moves in a safe, indoor environment until they are confident they can get them right outside.

David Belle

5

Training

The gym is the perfect place to work out new free-running moves before trying them outdoors. There are soft blocks to jump from and crash mats for falling safely. Free runners can bounce off **springboards** to give them the height to twist and spin. Foam pits are used to land in and to soften falls.

Many free-running moves have been invented in the gym.

a free runner building strength in his right arm

A free runner practising "the flag". This requires huge upper body and arm strength.

Free-running moves

David Belle and his friends created many basic free-running moves, developed from David's father's original moves and changed to work in the city. As the new sport spread, these moves were learnt by others, and they formed the basis of free running.

Drop

A fall or drop from a height with a smooth landing. Usually free runners bend their knees to take the impact and then go into a forward roll.

Scaling

When a free runner jumps straight at a wall. They place their front foot against the wall and then push upwards off this foot to climb higher than they could normally jump.

Guinness World Record for scaling: 3.49 metres

Gap jump

A jump between a gap – either two railings, two walls or over a stairwell. In this move especially, free runners have to make sure they jump carefully so they don't injure themselves.

10

Tic tac

Running up and across a wall, usually in order to get over an obstacle next to it.

11

Low vault

When a free runner vaults over railings, small walls or other obstacles in different ways. They can jump without using their hands to push themselves upwards, or use one hand, or both hands.

12

Some obstacles are too high for free runners to jump over using just their legs, but not high enough for them to need to climb a wall. For these obstacles, the free runner uses a high vault.

High vault

When a free runner mounts a high obstacle with their hands, and then pulls their legs and lower body over the obstacle.

13

Once their skills were perfected, David Belle and his friends liked the way that this new sport could take place anywhere. In Paris, they could use any ledge, roof, wall or piece of waste ground to practise free running. Suddenly, an ordinary **housing estate** was full of opportunities for jumps, leaps, twists and spins.

David's friend Sébastien Foucan named the sport "free running", because it was all about running freely, wherever they wanted to.

14

David Belle leaping from a building in a scene for a film

Another word for a free runner is "tracer". This is because as they run, a free runner traces a route through, over and around buildings.

This route can also be seen as a story with a beginning, a middle and an end. In this story, it's as if the free runner is running away from someone or something. There are obstacles in the way. The free runner overcomes them by demonstrating great skill. In a way, the free runner is both the storyteller and the hero in their own story.

Free-running fans

David and his group of free runners
continued to practise and film
their stunts. In 1997, they sent some
of their films to a French TV channel.
When the channel showed the stunts,
viewers were surprised by what the free
runners could do and wanted to see more.

Then the director Luc Besson decided to
use free running in a film starring
a group of free runners, including
David Belle, being chased by the police.
Nobody had seen anything like it before.
The sport quickly became popular, with
more people practising it to see for
themselves what they could do in
a city environment.

a boy filming his friend free running

What to wear

Free runners normally wear light clothing like a T-shirt with tracksuit bottoms or shorts.

For the free runner, the right shoes are very important. They need to be light and have an excellent grip. Many companies round the world now make shoes especially for the sport.

Free runners generally don't wear protective clothing. Most men and women practise the sport seriously, which means that they try to never take risks that are stupid or too dangerous. They use their experience to help them understand what moves might work, and they always work out and rehearse the moves beforehand, using a gym with lots of crash mats.

New moves

New free-running moves are being invented all the time. There are now over 100 well-known free-running moves.

Guinness World Record for farthest wall flip from a wall over a moving car: 3.04 metres

a free runner doing a wall flip

18

Aerial

A cartwheel performed without the free runner's hands touching the ground. The best free runners can add twists into this move.

19

Because free runners jump from roofs, vault stairwells and climb very high buildings, there can be injuries. But free running is like any sport – it needs training, focus and skill. In the films, the stunts always look sleek and polished. But each stunt would have been practised for many weeks, or even months.

Free runners know how important it is to train and to make sure they do not practise new stunts alone. Training is always done in pairs or groups. Free runners also know that they shouldn't let others dare them to go too far with moves they're not yet ready for.

Clubs and competitions

Many free runners join clubs where they can train and meet other fans. There are clubs all over the world and most free runners join when they are teenagers.

Free-running competitions take place throughout the year. These attract the best free runners from around the world.

Some of these competitions take place in arenas where sets are built for free runners to demonstrate their skills to packed audiences. These sets, like movie sets, are complete with buildings, towers, rooftops, railings, stairs and cars, ready for free runners to jump, leap and spin their way around them.

Pavels Petkuns performing in a competition in Greece

23

Famous free runners

Some free runners have become famous through their sport. One of the first ever free runners, Sébastien Foucan, was in the chase scene at the beginning of a James Bond film, and has also featured in one of Madonna's music videos.

Sébastien Foucan

As well as acting in movies, David Belle has helped to create movie stunts and has featured in music videos. Many companies have used free running in their adverts to promote products such as computers and TV channels.

There are many female free runners. Luci Steel Romberg is the most famous, and she is both a stuntwoman and the winner of many international free-running competitions.

Luci Steel Romberg

25

Free running around the world

Video-sharing sites have made it possible for free running to spread as a sport around the world, because people can watch the films online, no matter where they are. In Russia, free running is known as Russian Climbing. The sport is very popular in America, Europe, and South American countries such as Brazil.

The British free runner Ryan Doyle has toured to China, Japan, India and Jordan, filming fantastic stunts with local free runners.

Another British free runner, Damien Walters, has made films for video-sharing sites that have received over three million hits. Viewers like to watch the most dangerous and daring stunts, especially when free runners jump between very high buildings, or do backward flips off rooftops.

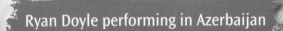

Ryan Doyle performing in Azerbaijan

The rapid rise of free running

From its beginnings in the 1980s in Paris, free running has grown into a popular and international sport. It is increasingly featured in films, video games and music videos, and many of the most talented free runners are now famous actors and stunt actors.

Because of this, the sport gains more free runners and more fans every year, and is practised in most major cities around the world. Free running has only existed for thirty years, but is considered to be one of the most exciting and fastest-growing extreme sports.

Glossary

housing estate an area with a large number of houses or flats built together

military to do with the armed forces: the navy, army and airforce

obstacles objects that are in your way and make it difficult to move forward

springboards strong boards that you jump on and use to help you jump high

stunts dangerous and difficult actions that somebody does to entertain people

vaulting jumping over an object in a single movement, using your hands or a pole to push you

Index

Being a free runner

clothing
Free runners wear light, comfortable clothing.

practising
Free runners practise their moves before using them on the street.

training
Free runners train safely in the gym.

new moves
Free runners invent new moves all the time.

filming
Free runners show their moves on video-sharing sites.

competitions
Competitions attract the best free runners in the world.

31

Ideas for reading

Written by Gillian Howell
Primary Literacy Consultant

Learning objectives: *(word reading objectives correspond with Lime band; all other objectives correspond with Ruby band)* continue to apply phonic knowledge and skills as the route to decode words until automatic decoding has become embedded and reading is fluent; drawing inferences and justifying inferences with evidence; retrieve and record information from non-fiction; asking questions to improve their understanding of a text

Curriculum links: P.E.

Interest words: obstacles, gymnastics, dangerous, vaulting, buildings, environment, scaling, rehearse, audiences

Word count: 1,514

Resources: whiteboard, pens, paper, art materials

Getting started

- Read the title together and ask the children if they have heard of free running and know what it is. Have they ever seen anyone doing it in films or in real life?

- Discuss the cover photograph with the children. Ask them to describe what the person in the photo is doing.

- Ask the children to predict what they will find out about free running in the book and make a note of their ideas on the whiteboard.

Reading and responding

- Ask the children to read the text aloud quietly. Listen in as they read and prompt as necessary. Remind them to use their phonic knowledge and contextual clues to help them read words they are unsure of.

- Remind the children to read the captions to the photos. As they read, ask them to make a note of the different types of free-running moves they encounter.

- Pause occasionally to check the children understand what they are reading, e.g. on p17, ask why the right sort of shoes are important for free running.

- Ask the children to read to the end of the book. Praise them for reading with fluency and support them when necessary.